A full explanation of day to day HR activities.

Price: £9.99

ISBN 978-1-4710-4534-9

HR in 5 Days

Pijush Sen

HR

Human Resource in 5 days

By

Pijush Sen

Diploma In Management

ISBN: 978-1-4710-4534-9

I devote this book to my wife Mala, daughter Mayukhi, and son Avighna.

CONTENTS AT A GLANCE

1 CONTENTS..5

2 INTRODUCTION..8

3 LITERATURE REVIEW OF RECRUITMENT AND SELECTION 10

4 CONTENT ANALYSIS OF STRATEGY STATEMENTS OF "ABC"
COMPANY FOR RECRUITMENT AND SELECTION..........................30

5 LITERATURE REVIEW OF REDEPLOYMENT..............................37

6 CONTENT ANALYSIS OF STRATEGY STATEMENTS OF "ABC"
COMPANY FOR REDEPLOYMENT..43

7 KEY QUESTIONS ASKED DURING "ABC" COMPANY INTERVIEW.......52

8 "XYZ" ACADEMY..54

9 ANNEX 1 56

10 BIBLIOGRAPHY..57

11 INDEX..58

1 Contents

1 CONTENTS..5

2 INTRODUCTION...8

2.1 FOCUS OF THE BOOK...8
2.2 BOOK BACKGROUND AND TERMS OF REFERENCE..8
2.3 BOOK APPROACH AND METHODOLOGY...9
   2.3.1 Literature review...9
   2.3.2 Content analysis of strategy statements...9
   2.3.3 Selected key interviews..9
2.4 BOOK STRUCTURE...9

3 LITERATURE REVIEW OF RECRUITMENT AND SELECTION 10

3.1 DEFINITION 10
3.2 PURPOSE OF RECRUITMENT AND SELECTION...11
3.3 RECRUITMENT FLOW CHART 12
   3.3.1 Part 1: Preliminary Stages..12
   3.3.2 Part 2: Interviewing and Selection Stages.......................................13
3.4 DEFINING REQUIREMENTS...14
   3.4.1 Requisition form..14
   3.4.2 Job descriptions..15
      3.4.2.1 Overall purpose..15
      3.4.2.2 Content..15
      3.4.2.3 Accountabilities..15
      3.4.2.4 Performance criteria..15
      3.4.2.5 Responsibilities 15
      3.4.2.6 Organizational factors...16
      3.4.2.7 Motivating factors...16
      3.4.2.8 Development factors...16
      3.4.2.9 Environmental factors..16
      3.4.2.10 Job specification form...17
   3.4.3 Person specifications..18
      3.4.3.1 Competence analysis..18
         3.4.3.1.1 Work-based or occupational competence 18
         3.4.3.1.2 Behavioural or personal competences 18
      3.4.3.2 Person specification form...19
3.5 ATTRACTING CANDIDATES..20
   3.5.1 Analysis of recruitment strengths and weakness...............................20
   3.5.2 A few points to attract candidates..21
      3.5.2.1 Good management..21
      3.5.2.2 Appropriate media...21
      3.5.2.3 Timing...21
      3.5.2.4 Eye-catching..21
      3.5.2.5 Sell the job..21
      3.5.2.6 Branding..21
      3.5.2.7 Salary details...21
      3.5.2.8 Include useful information..22

       3.5.3 Advertising..*22*

          3.5.3.1 Analyse the requirement.......................................23

          3.5.3.2 Write the copy..24

          3.5.3.3 Design the advertisement....................................24

          3.5.3.4 Plan the media...24

          3.5.3.5 Using executive search consultants.......................25

          3.5.3.6 Educational and training establishments.................25

    3.6 SELECTING CANDIDATES...26

       3.6.1 Sifting applications..*26*

          3.6.1.1 Recruitment control sheet....................................26

       3.6.2 Types of interview...*27*

       3.6.3 Assessment centres..*27*

       3.6.4 Interviewing arrangements......................................*27*

       3.6.5 Interviewing...*28*

       3.6.6 Selection tests...*28*

       3.6.7 References of others..*28*

       3.6.8 Induction and follow-up arrangements......................*29*

**4 CONTENT ANALYSIS OF STRATEGY STATEMENTS OF "ABC"
COMPANY FOR RECRUITMENT AND SELECTION**...............................**30**

    4.1 ESTABLISH THE BUSINESS NEED...30

    4.2 IDENTIFY THE JOB/DESCRIBE THE ROLE..................................30

    4.3 CLARIFY SKILLS AND COMPETENCIES REQUIRED.......................30

    4.4 ATTRACT CANDIDATES...31

    4.5 ASSESS AND SELECT..31

       4.5.1 Preparation...*31*

       4.5.2 Pre Selection...*32*

       4.5.3 Interview..*32*

       4.5.4 Decision...*32*

       4.5.5 Offer...*32*

    4.6 OFFER AND GAIN ACCEPTANCE..33

    4.7 INDUCTION PLAN..33

    4.8 STRENGTHS..34

    4.9 WEAKNESS...35

    4.10 COST AND BENEFITS...35

    4.11 RECOMMENDATIONS..36

5 LITERATURE REVIEW OF REDEPLOYMENT.................................**37**

    5.1 DEFINITION..37

    5.2 REDEPLOYMENT AND REDUNDANCY.....................................37

    5.3 PLANNING REDEPLOYMENT 37

    5.4 ALTERNATIVE TO REDEPLOYMENT 38

       5.4.1 Retraining *38*

       5.4.2 Secondment..*38*

    5.5 INVOLVING OTHERS...38

       5.5.1 Redeployment Pool..*38*

       5.5.2 Redeployment Committee.......................................*39*

       5.5.3 Redeployment Job Bank...*39*

    5.6 MONITORING REDEPLOYMENT 39

    5.7 DISMISSAL..40

       5.7.1 Fair reason for dismissal..*40*

5.7.2 Fair dismissal..41
5.7.3 The role of the individual manager..41
5.7.4 Analysing the dismissal case of the "XYZ" Academy...........................42

6 CONTENT ANALYSIS OF STRATEGY STATEMENTS OF "ABC" COMPANY FOR REDEPLOYMENT..43

6.1 REDEPLOYMENT PROCESS..43
6.1.1 Transfer and Change...43
6.1.2 Secondments...43
6.1.3 Changes to workforce type..44
6.2 REDUNDANCY PROCESS...45
6.2.1 Collective Consultation process..45
6.2.2 Role of an employee representative...45
6.2.3 Role of an employee...46
6.2.4 Voting process..46
6.2.5 Elected employee role...46
6.2.6 Employee Representative Nomination Form..47
6.2.7 Role of redundancy committee...48
6.2.8 Proposed selection criteria to be used...48
6.2.9 Proposed method of carrying out the redundancies and calculating termination arrangements...49
6.2.10 Outplacement Support..49
6.3 STRENGTHS...50
6.4 WEAKNESS..51
6.5 RECOMMENDATIONS..51

7 KEY QUESTIONS ASKED DURING "ABC" COMPANY INTERVIEW.......52

7.1 GENERAL..52
7.2 THE CHANGING ENVIRONMENT...52
7.3 THE BUSINESS PLAN...52
7.4 THE MANAGEMENT OF THE DEPARTMENT..52
7.5 LINKAGES...52
7.6 THE PROCESS OF PLANNING...53

8 "XYZ" ACADEMY...54

9 ANNEX 1 56

10 BIBLIOGRAPHY..57

11 INDEX..58

2 Introduction

2.1 Focus of the book

The book focuses on the policies statements in the management of the companies different departments and offices regarding recruitment and redeployment. Through an analysis of the content of policies statements and the process through which they are produced and implemented, the main elements needed to ensure effective policies statements are identified. Good practice examples are highlighted.   The importances of linking policies statements to business planning and resource allocation are identified. The book will conclude with a number of recommendations towards the future development and continuous development of policies statements.

2.2 Book background and terms of reference

Strategy statements are a central part of the Company's Strategic Management Initiative (SMI). As a formal expression of the strategic management process in the Company's departments and offices, strategy statements are intended to set out the key strategies and objectives to be achieved over a certain period.

As a relatively new initiative, strategy statements are still evolving. The intention is that they will encourage the adoption of a longer-term focus on strategic policy issues. But for the statements to operate effectively a number of questions need to be addressed. How are strategic priorities identified? To what extent should statements be drawn up in consultation with staff? How are unplanned and unexpected events dealt with? It is to address these and other related questions that the terms of reference for the book were determined. It book would aim to:

- Analyse the content and role of strategy statements, based on official documentation and legislation and discussions with key officials, and assess existing statements against their defined role.

- Review practice with regard to the role of strategy statements in the management of a cross section of a Company's departments and offices, focusing in particular on the linkages between strategy statements and business planning.

- Make recommendations as to the steps needed to ensure the effective use of strategy statements as a means of good strategic management practice.

2.3 Book approach and methodology

Three main sources of information were used in the book:

2.3.1 Literature review

The literature, both academic and from the company ("ABC"), was reviewed. This provided contextual material, plus information on the experience of other companies with strategic planning.

2.3.2 Content analysis of strategy statements

Strategy statements for the "ABC" departments and offices published in intranet were reviewed (see Annex 1 for a list of the strategy statements reviewed). These published statements provided insight into the practice of strategy statement preparation and the content areas covered in statements.

2.3.3 Selected key interviews

In order to obtain more in-depth information on the process of strategy statement preparation and the statements' impact to date, interviews took place with selected senior managers from the company's ("ABC") different departments.

2.4 Book structure

Section 3 explores the literature and reviews of Recruitment and Selection. Section 4 presents and reviews content analysis of strategy statements of "ABC" for Recruitment and Selection. "ABC" will be used as an anonymous company throughout this book. At the end of section 4, book has been discussed the strengths, weakness and cost-benefit analysis of Recruitment and Selection. At the end of section 4 recommendations made towards enhancing the impact of strategy statements in Recruitment and Selection of "ABC" procedure. The book also outlines a framework for the study, centred on three main concerns: the content of strategy statements; the process by which statements are derived and delivered; and the impacts and linkages which strategy statements are intended to have in practice. Section 5 explores the literature and reviews of Redeployment, Redundancy and Dismissal. Section 6 presents and reviews content analysis of strategy statements of "ABC" for Redeployment, Redundancy and Dismissal. At the end of section 6, book has been discussed the strengths, weakness and recommendations made towards enhancing the impact of strategy statements in Redeployment, Redundancy and Dismissal of "ABC" procedure. Section 7 listed all various questions asked to different departments managers during the Project Research. Section 9 is an annexure for a list of the strategy statements reviewed. Section 10 is last section and it is bibliography and listed all the references those have been studied for this book.

3   Literature Review of Recruitment and Selection

3.1   Definition

Recruitment and selection is a process for finding and employing people with the skills, experience, personality and attributes needed to do particular jobs competently and successfully, and with the potential to adapt their performance as the job demands develop or change. The three stages of recruitment and selection are:

- Defining requirements

    1. Preparing job descriptions

    2. Preparing specifications

    3. Deciding terms and conditions of employment

- Attracting candidates

    1. Reviewing and evaluating alternative sources of applicants inside and outside the company.

    2. Advertising

    3. Using agencies and consultants

- Selecting candidates

    1. Sifting applications

    2. Interviewing

    3. Testing

    4. Assessing candidates

    5. Assessment centres

    6. Offering employment

    7. Obtaining references

    8. Preparing contracts of employment

    9. Induction and follow-up arrangements

    10. Identification of good practice

    11. Identification of costs and benefits

    12. Improving the effectiveness of recruitment and selection

3.2 Purpose of recruitment and selection

- Employ the best person for a job.

- Comply with the equal opportunities policy.

- Attract the widest possible field of applicants.

- Give existing staff the chance to gain promotion.

- Bring new blood in the company from outside.

3.3   Recruitment flow chart

3.3.1   Part 1: Preliminary Stages

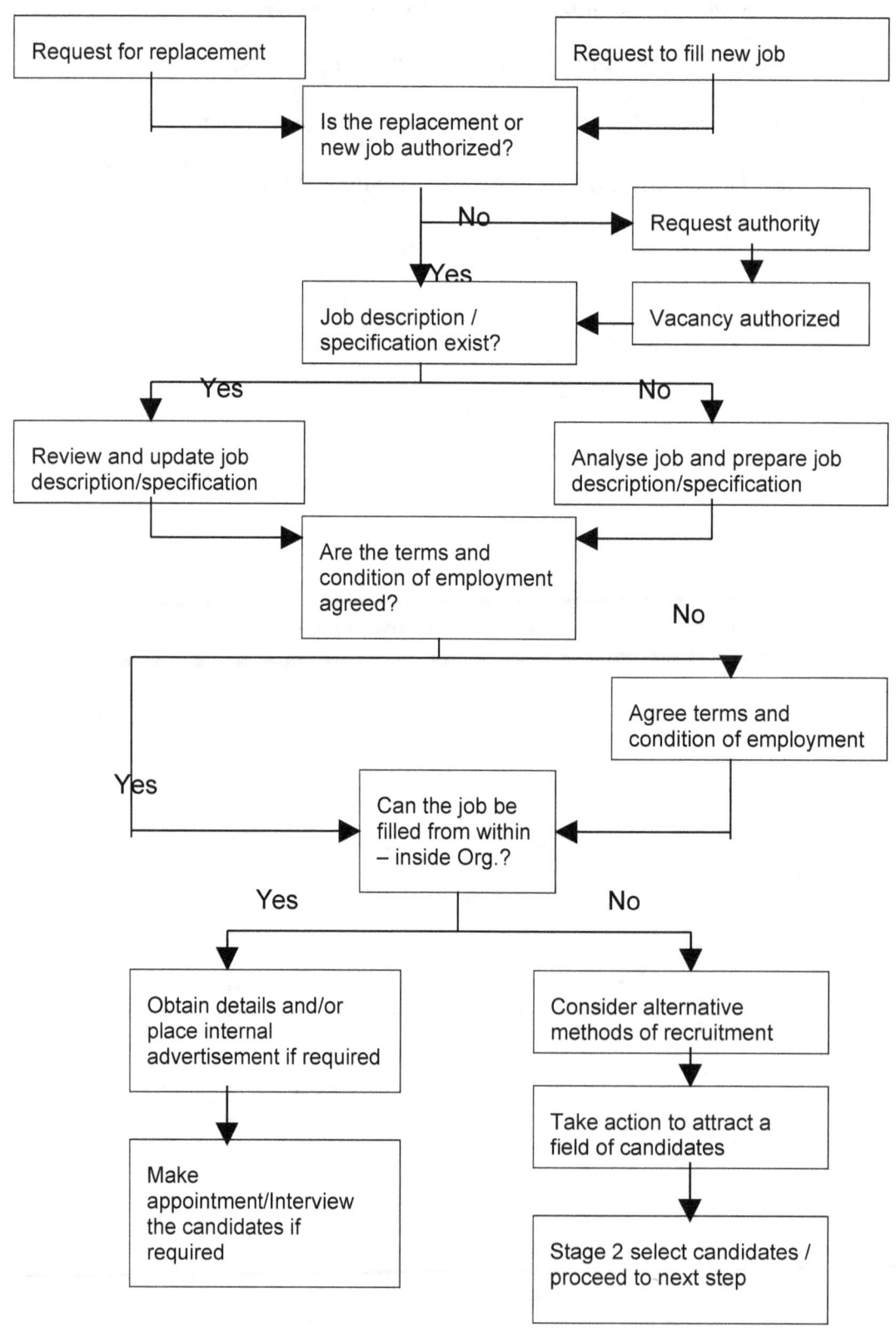

3.3.2 Part 2: Interviewing and Selection Stages

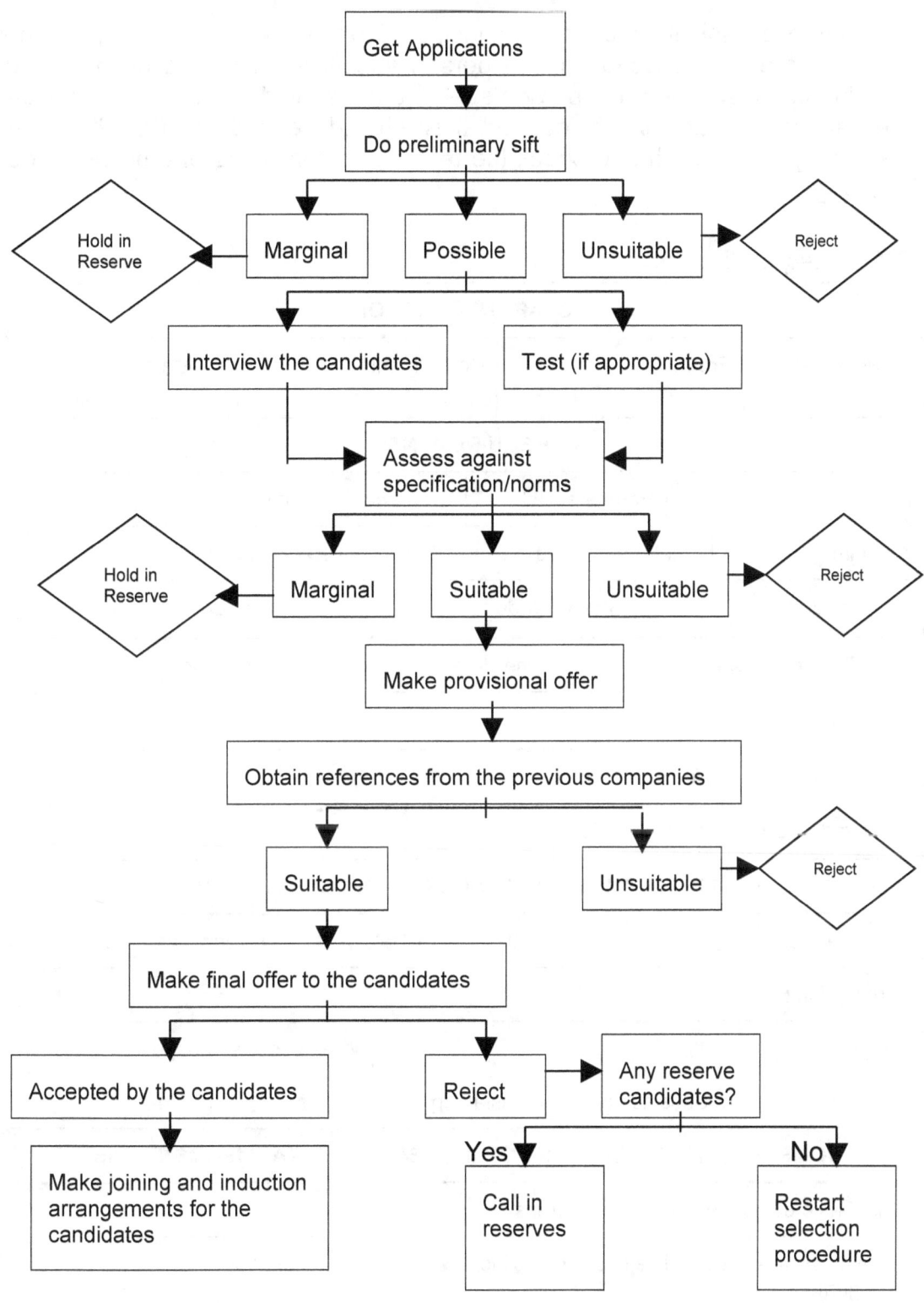

3.4 Defining requirements

In a large organization usually requisition form is available. If it were not available then job description and person specification should be prepared. Existing job description and person specification should be checked to ensure they are up to date and if required they should be updated first. It is also necessary to establish and check the terms and conditions of employment at this stage.

3.4.1 Requisition form

STAFF REQUISITION			
To Personal Department	From	Department	Date
REQUIREMENTS			
Job title	Permanent ☐	Contractor ☐ From	To
Age Limit	Qualification Req.		Experience Req.
Date needed	Salary Grade		Hours per day/wk
Over Time Applicable ☐	Overtime Rate		Manager Name
Work Experience			
Mandatory Business/Technical Skills			
Preferred Business/Technical Skills			
COMPLETE THE FOLLOWING FOR REPLACEMENT CASE			
Employee replaced	Job Title	Salary	Termination Date
Termination Reason			
Performance ☐ Above average ☐ Satisfactory ☐ Unsatisfactory		Would you re-engage? ☐ Yes ☐ No	
COMPLETE THE FOLLOWING FOR INCREASE IN ESTABLISHMENT CASE			
What has created the need for an increase?			
Explain why it is not possible to avoid this increase by organizational or other re-arrangements			
Increase in establishment approved ☐	Signed		Date

3.4.2 Job descriptions

A job description sets out the purpose of a job, where it fits in the organization structure, the context within which the job holder functions and the principal accountabilities of job holders, or the main tasks have to carry out (Armstrong, 1996). To prepare the job description the following information should be considered.

3.4.2.1 Overall purpose

Why the job exists and, in essence, what the job holder is expected to contribute for organization. For personnel director it would be, to advise on personnel strategies and policies and ensure that the personnel function provides the support required to implement them and that 'world class' personnel process are functioning effectively.

3.4.2.2 Content

The job content are the nature and scope of the job in terms of the tasks and operations to be performed and duties to be carried out – i.e. the processes of converting inputs (knowledge, skills and abilities) into outputs (results). For the personnel manager one of the key result areas would be provide a recruitment selection service to meet the companies needs Performance criteria.

3.4.2.3 Accountabilities

It is the result or outputs for which the job holder is accountable. For personnel director one of the principal accountabilities would be advise on employee relations and communications strategies and policies designed to maximize involvement and commitment while minimizing conflict.

3.4.2.4 Performance criteria

It is the criteria, measures or indicators, which enable an assessment to be carried out to ascertain the degree to which the job is being performed satisfactorily. For personnel manager one of the performance criteria would be a proactive approach is consistently adopted in making proposals to management on the development of personnel policies and practices which will improve business performance and add value.

3.4.2.5 Responsibilities

It is the level of responsibility the job holder has to exercise by reference to the scope and input of the job; the amount of discretion allowed to make decisions; the difficulty, scale, variety and complexity of the problems to be solved; the quality and value of the resources controlled; and the type and importance of interpersonal relations. One of the main responsibilities of personnel director would be formulate and implement personnel strategies, which are fully integrated with business strategies and cohere over all aspects of personnel management.

3.4.2.6 Organizational factors

It is the reporting relationships of the job holder, i.e. to whom he or she reports e.g. the line manager; the people reporting directly or indirectly to the job holder; and the extent to which the job holder is involved in teamwork. If the job holder is Personnel Officer then he would be reporting to Personnel Manager and Secretary would be reporting the job holder.

3.4.2.7 Motivating factors

It is the particular features of the job those are likely to motivate or demotivate job holders, if it is the demotivative then nothing is done about them.

3.4.2.8 Development factors

It is promotion and career prospects and the opportunity to acquire new skills or expertise during job holder career in the company.

3.4.2.9 Environmental factors

It is working conditions, health and safety considerations, unsocial hours, mobility, discrimination, and ergonomic factors relating to the design and use of equipment or workstations.

All these information regarding job descriptions have recorded on a job specification form on next page.

3.4.2.10   Job specification form

JOB SPECIFICATION	
Department name	Section/Project name
Job title / Designation	Job grade / Band
Reporting to (the line manager job title)	
Overall purpose of job / Contribution to organization	
Main activities / responsibilities / task	
Special requirements / Resource used (tools and equipment used, external contacts, etc)	
Other features of job: shift, night shift, overtime, work from home, travel, working conditions, etc	
Location of job	

3.4.3 Person specifications

Person specifications known as recruitment, personnel or job specifications, define the qualifications, experience, skills and competences require by the job holder and any other necessary information on the special demands made by the job, such as physical conditions, unusual hours, night work, overtime, or travel away from home. They also set out or refer to terms and conditions of employment such as pay, employee benefits, bonus, working hours, seek leaves and holidays. The information on the qualifications, work-based and behavioural competences would be derived from the competence analysis.

3.4.3.1 Competence analysis

Competence analysis is concerned with functional analysis to determine work-based competences such as job analysis and behavioural analysis to establish the behavioural dimensions that affect job performance such as achieving result.

3.4.3.1.1 Work-based or occupational competence

Which refer to expectations of workspace performance and expectations of what people have to be able to do if they are going to achieve the results required in the job, and the standards and outputs that people carrying out specified roles are expected to attain – these are the areas of competence, which will be expressed in terms of outputs and the standards of performance they must reach in all the job's main elements (Armstrong, 1996). Some competences would be: interviewing techniques, job analysis, administrating fairly complex paperwork processes, inputting data to computers.

3.4.3.1.2 Behavioural or personal competences

Which refer to the personal characteristics and behaviour required for successful performance in such areas as interpersonal skills, leadership, personal drive, communication skills, team membership and analytical ability (Armstrong, 1996). Some competences would be: able to relate well to others and use interpersonal skills to achieve desired objectives, able to influence behaviour and decisions of people on matters concerning recruitment and other personal and individual issues, able to cope with change, to be flexible and to handle uncertainty, able to maintain appropriately directed energy and stamina to exercise self-control and to learn new behaviours.

These information regarding person specifications have recorded on person specification form on next page.

3.4.3.2 Person specification form

PERSON SPECIFICATION		
Educational qualifications and special training			
Experience		
Work-based competences (Technical skills, business knowledge, functional knowledge etc)		
Essential	Desirable
Behavioural competences (Leader ship, communication, impact and influence, team work etc)		
Essential	Desirable

3.5 Attracting candidates

Attracting candidates is primarily a matter of identifying, evaluating and using the most appropriate sources of applicants. However, in case where difficulties in attracting or retaining candidates are being met or anticipated, it may be necessary to carry out a preliminary study of the factors that are likely to attract or repel candidates – the strengths and weakness of the organization as an employer (Armstrong, 1996).

3.5.1 Analysis of recruitment strengths and weakness

The analysis of strengths and weakness should cover such matters as the national or local reputation of the organization, pay, employee benefits and working conditions, the basic interest of the job, security of employment, opportunities for education and training, career prospects, and the location of the office or plant. These need to be compared with the competition and selling-points can be drawn up as in a marketing exercise, in which the preferences of potential customers are compared with the features of the product e.g. quality, price which are likely to provide most appeal to the customers. Candidates are also selling themselves, but they are also buying what the organization has to offer. In latter sense, the labour market is a buyer's market, the company is selling itself to candidates, must study their needs in relation to what it can provide.

A study can be used to prepare a better image of the organization for use in advertisements, brochures or interviews. The company can point out where the organization needs to improve as an employer if it is to attract more or better candidates and to retain those selected. The study could make use of an attitude survey to obtain the views of existing employees.

Once an engineering company surveyed the market and were written special brochures for each major discipline giving technical case histories of the sort of work graduates carried out. The main concern of the brochures to attract university graduates that they can developed the knowledge they gained at university and proved to be most useful recruitment aid.

3.5.2 A few points to attract candidates

3.5.2.1 Good management

It is important to conduct recruitment and recruitment advertising within an effective framework. It should have a resourcing plan; a clear understanding of the company needs and the marketplace; and an excellent working partnership with external suppliers.

3.5.2.2 Appropriate media

The employers should emphasise the importance of identifying the most appropriate media for the vacancy filled. It should ensure adverts are placed in appropriate media for the type of vacancy, e.g. grade, skilled, semi-skilled, professional.

3.5.2.3 Timing

The timetable of the recruitment and selection process needs to be carefully planned. The advertisement should appear at a suitable time; this involves consideration of the frequency of the publication concerned and when readers are likely to see the advert.

3.5.2.4 Eye-catching

Advertisement must attract the attention of casual readers. It needs to be eye-catching in design and wording.

3.5.2.5 Sell the job

Depending on the organization's needs, it may be necessary to be upbeat in tone and avoid precise criteria. When placing ads, it should be precise as possible in what type of person the company is looking for and what qualifications are required.

3.5.2.6 Branding

Advertising can be more effective where an employer already has an established brand (a reputation). If appropriate, recruitment advertising can be used to build a brand. In other cases, it must adhere to an established corporate branding policy. Advertising must be carefully targeted, with right brands and messages.

3.5.2.7 Salary details

Their inclusion is controversial, but evidence shows it improves effectiveness. The best way to attract applicants has been those adverts, which include the pay rate/salary.

3.5.2.8 Include useful information

It should include contact details like contact person, other key selection information and clear closing date.

3.5.3 Advertising

The Company should look for candidates within the company to fill up the vacancy, if there is no one available then company policy should be advertise vacancy externally as well as internally. The job title is the most important factor for jobseekers at senior level, closely followed by salary.

The advertisement should emphasise on these following points:

- The requirements of the job.

- The necessary and the desirable criteria for job applicants.

- The activities and working practise of the organization.

- The job location.

- The reward package.

- Job tenure (eg contract length).

- The application procedure.

The main sources of candidates are:

- Advertising on different media

- Recruitment Agencies

- Recruitment consultants

- Executive search consultants

- Educational establishments

The objective of an advertisement should be:

- Attract attention – it must complete for the interest of potential candidates against other employees.

- Create and maintain interest – It has to communicate in attractive and interesting way information about the job, the company, the terms and conditions of employment and the qualifications required.

- Stimulate action – the message needs to be conveyed in a manner, which will not only focus people's eyes on advertisement but also encourage them to read the end, as well as prompt a sufficient number of replies from good candidates.

To achieve these criteria, it should complete the following section:

- Analyse the requirement

- Decide who does what

- Write the copy

- Design the advertisement

- Plan the media

- Evaluate the response

3.5.3.1 Analyse the requirement

First check how many jobs have to be filled and by when and then check the job descriptions and person specifications to obtain information on responsibilities, qualifications and experience required and any other information needed to draft the advertisement.

The next step is to consider where suitable candidates are likely to come from; the companies, jobs or education establishments they are in; and the parts of the country where they can be found and depends on this advertisement media can planned.

Finally, think about what is likely to attract candidates about the job or the company so the most can be made of these factors in the advertisement. Analyse previous success or failures to establish what does or does not work is another area to think about to do better this time.

3.5.3.2 Write the copy

A recruitment advertisement should start with a convincing headline and it should have this information:

- Organization name

- Job title

- Qualification and experience required for the job

- Payments and benefits

- Job location

- Action to be taken

The job title should be in bold type and quote the salary and point out all the benefits e.g. car, bonus. If the organization wants to be anonymous then it should use a consultant. Advertisement should include any selling points e.g. growth or diversification, and any other areas of interest of a potential candidates e.g. career prospects.

Advertisement must not discriminate the candidates, it should not include job titles as 'salesman' or 'stewardess', and it should include neutral title such as 'sales representative'.

The advertisement should end with information how candidates can apply for the job, they should have permission to write, make telephone calls for any information.

3.5.3.3 Design the advertisement

- For managerial, technical and professional jobs full display advertisement would be appropriate. They are bordered; any typeface and illustration can be used. They are expensive but have more meaningful impact on candidates.

3.5.3.4 Plan the media

- For managerial, professional jobs 'quality papers' would be the best.

- Nowadays Internet is most popular for any kind of advertisement. For managerial, professional jobs reputed and well-known Internet site can be used.

3.5.3.5 Using executive search consultants

They can be used for senior position. They are called as 'head hunter' and charge 30 – 50% of the first year salary. A few guidelines to choose them are:

- Reputation

- Type of jobs the consultancy deals

- Meet the consultant to assesses his or her quality

- Compare fees

3.5.3.6 Educational and training establishments

Graduate recruitment is a major exercise for some companies. They visit the college/university campuses to recruit the graduate and postgraduate students. For senior position organization should target well-known university for campus interview and recruit candidates from there.

3.6 Selecting candidates

3.6.1 Sifting applications

The steps required to process and sift applications is as follows:

- List the applications in a recruitment control sheet given below.

- Compare all the applications against the job specification and categories in three categories suitable, marginal and unsuitable.

- The possible candidates list should be scrutinize by the manager and draw up a short list. The list should have four to eight candidates.

- Draw up an interview programme. For a senior position sixty minutes or more would be required.

- Review the remaining possible and marginal candidates and decide if any of them are to be held in reserve. Send reserves a standard 'holding' letter and send others a standard rejection letter.

3.6.1.1 Recruitment control sheet

Ref			Vacancy							
Media										
No.	Media Ref	Name	Address	Suitable	Unsuitable	Marginal	Acknowledge	Interview Result	Grade	Final letter

3.6.2 Types of interview

For senior job position individual interviews or interviewing panels can be used. Individual interview is a face-to-face interview. Interviewing panels is where two more people gather together to interview one candidate.

3.6.3 Assessment centres

Assessment centre is a more comprehensive approach to selection. This has the following features.

- The centre focuses on behaviour.

- Exercise like one-to-one role-plays, 'in-tray' exercises and group exercise are included to simulate the key dimensions of the job. Performance in these simulations predicts behaviour on the job.

- Interviews and other tests like psychometric, aptitude, reasoning and personality test used in addition group exercise.

- Performance is measured in terms of competencies required for the job role.

- Several candidates are assessed together to allow interaction and to make the experience more open and participative.

- Senior managers are involved in assessing.

- From personality test the company can match personal profile for the required job role.

3.6.4 Interviewing arrangements

- The candidate should know in advance where to come and whom to ask for and interview time

- The waiting place for candidate should be quite and comfortable with reading materials, and access to cloakroom and canteen facilities

3.6.5 Interviewing

Structured and behaviourally based interviews would appropriate for strategic management job role. The aim of this interview assesses the candidate against the competency required by the job role. A few typical questions would be like this.

- Describe a situation in which the candidate persuaded others to take an unusual course of action.

- Describe an occasion when the candidate completed a task in the face of great difficulties.

- Describe any contribution the candidate has made as a member of a team in achieving a successful result.

- Describe any situation in which the candidate took the lead in getting something worthwhile done.

- Has candidate set a vision for the previous company?

3.6.6 Selection tests

Personality test would be appropriate to select candidate for strategic management job role. It gives a picture of candidate's behaviour, organization, co-ordination and how they interact with the environment. There are different personality tests. These include self-report personality questionnaires and other questionnaires, which measures interests, values or work behaviour.

3.6.7 References of others

After the interviewing and testing procedure has been completed a provisional decision should be taken to offer by telephone or writing. Before offering satisfactory references should be taken. One or two candidates should be hold in reserve. After satisfactory references have been obtained offer should be confirmed.

3.6.8 Induction and follow-up arrangements

Whenever there is new one joining at senior level on company intranet it should be announced. The candidate should have been given all necessary information to settle down quickly in new environment.

When employee arrives at first day, responsible person should welcome him. He should be given employee handbook and other necessary documents e.g. bank details form, where the monthly package will be deposited.

There should be departmental induction, which will explain him all necessary information about the job and how to take handover.

It is essential to follow up newly engaged employees to ensure that they have settled down and they are doing well. It is always better to find out the problem at early stage. Follow-up will ensure it is a best fit for the job role, and if there is any mistake it should be identified to do better next time. Follow-up will help in continuous improvement in recruitment and selection.

4 Content analysis of strategy statements of "ABC" company for Recruitment and Selection

It got seven steps to select a candidate:

1. Establish the business need

2. Identify the job/describe the role

3. Clarify skills and competencies required

4. Attract candidates

5. Assess and select

6. Offer and gain acceptance

7. Induction plan

4.1 Establish the business need

Usually recruitment is initiated for one or two reasons, either as a result of business growth/expansion changes in the need of customer, or to replace some one who is leaving the company or transferring to a new role. The manager should identify the 'best fit' generic job(s) from the "ABC" organization Map. The position should be posted onto intranet. The requirements and business justification should be produced, and others alternatives should be analysed.

4.2 Identify the job/describe the role

The generic job description is available on the company intranet for selection manager. The manager should identify which job description is suitable for the candidate.

4.3 Clarify skills and competencies required

For every generic job role required competencies and skills are available on the company intranet. The manager should match the candidate's profile for the required competencies and skills.

4.4 Attract candidates

It is the company policy to source the candidate internally wherever possible. Vacancies are advertised internally except when the managing director or resource director decides that this is not appropriate. The company has a predetermined list of preferred suppliers with agreed fee rates and terms and conditions of business.

- The Manager can agree a recruitment campaign plan with the HR Recruitment Manager, which will include the following:

- Method of attracting suitable candidates (advertising / agency database etc.)

- Budget and all costs associated with the method.

- The selection process itself (ie. Content of the interview / tests / presentations etc)

- Diary timetable clearly outlining who is involved in the process and when they will need to be available for interviewing

4.5 Assess and select

Assessment and selection considered in five stages

- Preparation

- Pre Selection

- Interview

- Decision

- Offer

4.5.1 Preparation

- The manager should read all the paperwork including the CV. In the case the candidate is internal or formal employees the HR helpdesk will provide access to historical data (appraisals, personal files, termination reports, psychometric test or assessments).

- He should prepare fact-finding questions on work experience, knowledge and skills.

- He should design all questions to seek out evidence of preferred behaviour according to competencies.

- He should list a number of probing questions to quality information.

- He should prepare he has the correct number of interview data packs.

4.5.2 Pre Selection

Comparing information from application forms or CV against job descriptions and skill requirements can do pre-selection.

For senior position an initial telephone discussion may be arranged to establish mutual interest.

4.5.3 Interview

For a one-hour interview, plan would be like this:

1. Welcome and rapport building for two minutes

2. Introduction to the interview for two minutes

3. Gathering information

    - Check questions / personnel circumstances for five minutes

    - Experience / knowledge / job motivation for fifteen minutes

    - Skills and competencies for twenty minutes

4. Giving information for ten minutes

5. Selling and closing for five minutes

4.5.4 Decision

All persons involved in the assessment and selection step should pool the information gathered before you come to a decision on recruitment.

4.5.5 Offer

After decision has been made about the candidate the next step is making offer to the candidate.

4.6 Offer and gain acceptance

It is essential the manager should move speedily and effectively to ensure the offer is made and acceptance obtained. The manager should make final by taking references and medical clearance. The written offer would be made within two working days of the decision. The offer should state the "ABC" official job title from the organization map and it should have a date by which response must be received and during this period the manager will contact the candidate to clarify any issues.

The manager should give feedback to all internal and external candidates if they seek. The candidates the manager turns down could be or could influence customers or employees of the future. Their only impression of "ABC" can be formed from the way in which their application has been handled.

4.7 Induction plan

Successful recruitment can be undermined by poor induction – the cost of retaining people is invariably far cheaper than having to spend money on further recruitment. Induction will introduces the candidate with the job, the people, the business, the facilities, and the company systems, processes and procedures.

A well-planned induction helps the integration of an employee, maximising morale through early success and quickly raising the level of performance. It is equally important for both the external and the internal recruit – both have things they need to know if they are to contribute effectively.

After the individual has accepted the offer will go through group induction process and conduct the new employees in order to:

- Welcome and support the decision to join "ABC"

- Indicate when, where and how to commence work

- Arrange a visit to meet future colleagues and to discuss any handover arrangements

- Indicate any changes, which have occurred subsequent to selection, which could affect the job

- Confirm any agreement to honour holiday arrangements

Before new employee arrives it should be ensured everyone who needs to know has been informed.

4.8 Strengths

1. It gives opportunity to internal candidates promotion and career development.

2. It says managers how to establish recruitment within the budget.

3. The company has every generic job role description and person specification for every generic job role; these are available on intranet and in Lotus Notes database.

4. It uses effectively time of HR managers, because it advises to follow pre-defined steps for recruitment and selection.

5. It has clear and objective criteria to measure and compare candidates. It advises managers how to prepare for interview and use different assessment methods to assess candidates depending on the job role.

6. It says managers use planned questions against skill and competency criteria to judge the candidate.

7. It uses executive search consultants' method to get candidates reference; it is a confidential method.

8. It reduces employee turnover and recruitment cost, because it selects right candidates for job roles at end who will be stable.

9. It improves quality of service to customers, because it selects right candidates for jobs role at end.

10. For senior positions eg General Manager, Director it uses initial telephone discussion to establish mutual interest.

11. For rejected candidates it provides feedback, because they could influence customers or employees of the future.

12. It has good induction plan, which helps to retain candidates.

4.9 Weakness

- Present method is not simple, because it goes though different steps and procedures.

- The HR department and managers need to put much time and enough resource for this method.

- This method may not get enough time to select a candidate within the old employee notice time.

- If a replacement need immediately or a candidate need urgently this procedure may not get it done quickly.

- It uses different kind of agency for candidates source, these agency charge a large amount of money for a candidate who is selected from their source.

- Present recruitment and selection method does not say for different generic job roles what type of questions managers should ask candidates to evaluate skills and competency.

4.10 Cost and benefits

- The company recruitment and selection methods retain people for a long-term; retaining person is invariably far cheaper than having to spend money on further recruitment.

- It goes through very complex procedure but at end it selects right candidates. It puts the cost at front but it end up with select right candidate. This procedure cannot select a misfit because unsuitable candidates will be filtered out at some stage. If an unsuitable candidate gets select it cost lots more to company and its customers and company image as well.

- If there is a need to select General Manager or Director who are level above of the personnel manager of the HR department then it can take help of executive search consultants who will give the correct information about the candidate. Based on those information and formal interview it can select General Manager or Director. This method would be costly because they charge up to 50% basic annual salary but in long-term it is cost-effective. Because General Managers or Directors are important to company and they take the company to reach visions.

4.11 Recommendations

- It will be helpful for managers if it says specifically which assessment criteria is appropriate for what type of job roles.

- It will be helpful for managers if they know what are the questions need to be asked to evaluate skills and competency of candidates for job roles.

- It should advertise vacancies to well known Internet site. Presently it advertises on own Internet site.

- For senior positions and highly senior positions (GM, Director) it should advertise jobs on well-known national newspapers.

- When the company advertise jobs on own Internet site it should include salary, benefits, because these factors attracts candidate first. Presently it does not do that.

- It should forecast how many employee need for next year and should visit reputed college/university campus for recruitment and selection.

5 Literature Review of Redeployment

5.1 Definition

The key elements of the redeployment policy are the establishment of a process for identification of surplus staff seeking redeployment together with the identification of vacant positions considered suitable for redeployment.

Redeployment means the re-assignment of a staff member whose position has been declared redundant into a suitable vacant position. Redeployment may involve the staff member's re-assignment to a position located at another location of unit.

5.2 Redeployment and Redundancy

Redeployment is not always associated with redundancy. Having a proper redeployment policy in place will facilitate redeployment to a more viable situation quickly and efficiently without causing undue stress and disturbance. In these situations the redundancy provisions would be ignored in favour of the redeployment options. However departments would need to be certain that there is no possibility of redundancy in the new position before proceeding.

5.3 Planning redeployment

At the time of deciding that there are justifiable reasons for possible staff reductions a strategy needs to be developed to explore all the options available before resorting to the ultimate remedy of redundancy.

In the initial stages managers are advised to proceed with caution in discussing the matter of possible redundancies with their staff. While general discussion in respect to the needs of the particular work unit may proceed in broad terms, there should be no indication to individual staff that their jobs may be redundant. It is accepted that this may be extremely difficult in small units, however a sensitive approach and a greater emphasis on the alternatives to redundancy referred to below may help reduce the impact on staff.

The Unions may raise serious concerns on occasions regarding the premature and inappropriate advice to some staff that their jobs will be redundant, when in fact no such decisions had been made.

The redundancy process is an extremely upsetting and stressful time for staff whose jobs have been identified as surplus. Managers should treat such staff with great support, sympathy and tact.

The HR should be contacted if, at the appropriate time, managers feel that they require some assistance or support in advising surplus staff that their position is no longer required.

When redundancy become the only solution, a timetable and processes for offering of a voluntary separation in accordance with the company Bargaining Agreement will need to be developed and made available to all staff.

The senior manager like Director will give the ultimate advice to staff regarding their impending redundancy.

5.4 Alternative to redeployment

Staff in areas where numbers need to be reduced may be offered alternatives to redundancy such as:

- Voluntary separation
- Voluntary retrenchment
- Conversion to partial appointment
- Redeployment
- Secondment
- Retraining

Redundancies should only be considered when there are no other options.

5.4.1 Retraining

The option to undertake appropriate retraining should be provided, either internally or externally, to equip a potentially surplus staff member with suitable skills to enable them to be usefully and viably employed by the company either by the same work unit or as a redeployee within another unit of the company.

5.4.2 Secondment

The opportunity for secondment both internally and externally should be encouraged although this is not considered an effective long-term solution.

5.5 Involving others

5.5.1 Redeployment Pool

Staff whose jobs have been declared redundant may elect to be included in a redeployment pool for possible appointment to another vacant position. A staff member nominating for the redeployment pool will be required to submit a current resume listing skills, qualifications, competencies, personal attributes and any other relevant information to the Redeployment Committee for inclusion in the Pool

5.5.2 Redeployment Committee

A committee consisting of:

- The Director or Deputy Director

- Recruitment Manager

- Employee Relations Manager

- Job Evaluation Manager

- Relevant Union representative as observe

Will be responsible for initial selection and nomination of surplus staff members for vacant positions.

5.5.3 Redeployment Job Bank

Vacant positions, which have been approved for filling, will be registered with the Redeployment Job Bank for matching by the Redeployment Committee with a surplus staff member from the Redeployment Pool. Staff from the Redeployment Pool will have first priority in respect to any vacancy before the position is advertised.

5.6 *Monitoring Redeployment*

1. The Redeployment Committee will assess the skills and attributes of staff members in the redeployment pool against the selection criteria for the particular position to be filled.

2. Positions are not to be advertised or filled until a search for potential candidates within the Redeployment Pool has been completed. Priority in filling any position must be given to redeployees.

3. Where a suitable candidate is found details will be forwarded to the relevant Unit for perusal with a strong recommendation from the Redeployment Committee that the employee be given a trial period. Any placement will be subject to consultation with the relevant Director or Deputy Director Administration.

4. The staff member will be advised by the Redeployment Committee of the details of the vacant position and the relevant Manager to contact for commencement arrangements.

5. The vacant position will be subject to a twelve weeks trial period for some staff, and six months for some staff. In the event of the staff member proving unsatisfactory for the position, the Manager must submit a report to the Redeployment Committee stating the reasons for unsuitability. In this situation or where the position has proved unsuitable for the employee, they may be referred to the Redeployment Committee for further re-assignment to another suitable position.

6. Where redeployment is not possible, redundancy provisions will apply.

7. The period of time in the Redeployment Pool will be considered part of the notice period referred to in the Redundancy provisions of the company Agreement.

5.7 Dismissal

An employee will be treated as dismissed if:

- The employer with or without notice terminates their contract.

- A fixed-term contract expires without being renewed under the same contract.

- The employee terminates the contract with or without notice because of the employers conduct.

- The employer refuses to allow a woman to exercise her right to return to work after maternity leave.

5.7.1 Fair reason for dismissal

Under the Employment Rights Act 1996 there are five potentially fair reasons for dismissal.

1. A lack of capability or qualification to carry out the work employed for.

2. Unsatisfactory conduct.

3. Redundancy.

4. Continuing to work would contravene a statue.

5. Some other substantial reason.

5.7.2 Fair dismissal

Dismissal will only be fair if following points mentioned below have been followed:

- Dismissal was for one of the above five reasons.

- A discipline procedure has been followed – if appropriate.

- Employee was given a chance to improve performance or conduct (except in cases of gross misconduct).

- Employee has been given a chance to explain the reasons for his behaviour.

- Employees appeal has been heard – if exercised.

5.7.3 The role of the individual manager

Often, the only person possessing formal power to dismiss is the organisation's chief executive, although he or she will obviously be guided by the advice of others. The manager might be expected to draft regulations, determine standards of behaviour and job performance, determine standards of behaviour and job performance, interpret rules imposed by higher management, clarify 'custom and practice' in relation to unwritten rules and explain to employees the firm's expectations of their behaviour. Almost certainly, the manager will have to negotiate with workers' representatives (usually union representatives) when disciplinary problems arise and must therefore be fully conversant with the details of company rules and procedures as well as the facts of individual cases.

Serious difficulties can arise from conflicting pressures on managers put forth by different departments in respect of disciplinary issues. The personnel departments, for instance, might want you to ignore a union work place representative are persistent late coming or absence because of the industrial relations difficulties that disciplining this employee might create. Senior managers may overturn his/her decisions. Deals might be struck between the personnel officer and union representatives behind his/her back. Other sections may fear the consequences of disrupted production schedules should you take action against certain individuals. Yet, it is the executive manager, not others, who must live with the detrimental effects of indiscipline. Colleague may not appreciate the practical problems created by absence, persistent late coming, petty pilfering, deliberate idling, messing about, etc.

5.7.4 Analysing the dismissal case of the "XYZ" Academy

The dismissal case of the "XYZ" (anonymous) Academy document has been enclosed at the section 8 of this book.

After careful review of the facts presented in the case study in relation to dismissal of Mr. Nobert I have reached to the following decisions mentioned below. I have paid particular regard to the ACAS Code of Practice on Disciplinary and Grievance Procedures, Sept 2000.

- No formal disciplinary hearing took place.

- Although two warnings were issued in writing to Mr. Nobert (the employee), the wording and format of those were inadequate. They omitted to make explicit that dismissal would be one of the consequences of a continuing failure to improve (ACAS Section 1, 9 i & 9 vi).

- Two warnings were issued in writing to Mr. Nobert were not filed.

- Mr. Nobert was provided with an inadequate opportunity to state his case at the senior management level before the dismissal decision was reached (ACAS Section 1, 9 ix).

- Mr. Nobert was not informed of his right to be accompanied (ACAS Section 1, 9 x).

- There was a lack of rigorous investigation into Mr. Nobert's conduct (ACAS Section 1, 9 vii).

- Mr. Nobert was not provided with a recommended right of appeal to a more senior manager (ACAS Section 1, 9 xiv).

- No consideration was given to a brief period of paid suspension ('cooling off period') (ACAS Section 1, 13).

- Mr. Nobert was not offered training or other support to help him improve his level of performance.

6 Content analysis of strategy statements of "ABC" company for Redeployment

6.1 Redeployment process

Employees classed as 'benched' are first priority for redeployment. The approach to resource allocation and management will support corporate and business strategy and objectives. There is a common consistent Skill Data Definition model to describe skill sets, role definitions, Industry sectors, Functional areas and Technology. The matching process will take into account the required skills, experience, sector knowledge, location, individual preferences, rates and availability. The methodology to transfer employees either within the business unit or between business units will be consistent with existing procedures for Transfer, Secondment, and Change in Workforce Type.

6.1.1 Transfer and Change

During the course of their employment with the Company the employee may transfer between different departments or projects, and, as a result, report into a different Line Manager.

- Transfers of employees are subject to the needs of the business at that time.

- Where an employee moves/is moved for a significant period of time to address a long-term business needs this is deemed to be a transfer.

- Where an employee moves/is moved to address an immediate or short time business need, or to address a short-term development need this is deemed to be a Secondment.

6.1.2 Secondments

A secondment is where an employee performs a role on a temporary basis as a result of a business need or to aid the employee's personal development.

- Secondments outside the Company will require approval as per the Company's Approval Matrix.

- The employee will continue to be career managed by their current ('home') Line Manager, but for the duration of the secondment they will be line managed by the person that they report to in the 'host' project/department/organisation.

- The employee's 'home' project/department Line Manager will be responsible for finding the employee a new role once the secondment ends.

- Typically a secondment will be for up to 6 - 12 months. However, there may be a business need why this should be longer. If the employee is moving permanently to the new role the transfer (and change) process should normally be followed.

- Secondments within Enterprise Solutions cannot exceed one month in duration before a transfer is effected.

6.1.3 Changes to workforce type

Individuals may change between different contractual arrangements during the course of their association with the Company. Where this happens it is known as a change to workforce type, examples of which are listed below:

1. An employee on a part time contract changing to one on full time hours

2. An <u>FEC</u> employee changing to part time or full time hours

3. A full time employee changing to part time hours

4. An employee on a Temporary Employment Contract changing to a permanent contract or vice versa

5. A contractor changing to a permanent contract or vice versa.

- Any changes in workforce type are driven by the needs of the business

- A change in workforce type must comply with the Workforce Relationship Principles Matrix

- Changes in workforce type require approval as per the Company's Approval Matrix

6.2 Redundancy process

6.2.1 Collective Consultation process

Any employer proposing redundancies of 20 or more staff in a single establishment within a 90-day period is required by employment legislation to inform and consult with employee representatives about these redundancies.

Collective redundancy consultation is designed to facilitate debate about ways to avoid potential redundancies altogether, reduce the numbers to be affected or lessen the impact to individuals and the Company.

Consultation must take place before the employer takes any final decisions about redundancies. It should be undertaken with the objective of agreement between the Company and the employee representatives.

Sufficient information must be provided by the Company to assist employee representatives to properly understand the redundancy proposals, background and reasons for them. Typically, this information will include:

- A statement about the redundancies and the reasons for them.

- Details of the numbers of employees likely to be affected by the redundancies and their roles.

- The proposed criteria to be used to select employees for redundancy and details of the proposed method of dismissal.

- How any non-statutory redundancy payments will be calculated.

For this period of Collective Redundancy Consultation, "ABC" seeks representatives from the areas likely to be impacted, Business Change, Enterprise Solutions, Systems Integration and Corporate Functions. A total of about ten employee representatives would be sought for 100 redundant employees.

6.2.2 Role of an employee representative

Employee representatives provide a communication channel between employees and the Business and HR Managers in their area of the business.

During the consultation period they are responsible for consulting with and capturing the views of employees on ways and means of avoiding or reducing the numbers of redundancies.

Following this period, representatives will meet with the HR team to ensure all views are fully reflected in the final report.

Representatives do not see the names of those selected for potential redundancy and are not responsible for challenging or supporting individual cases.

6.2.3 Role of an employee

To seek election as an employee representative in "ABC" for this period of collective redundancy consultation, you will need to:

- Be employed by "ABC", now and throughout the consultation period, and

- Be in a Business Unit for which we seek representation so as to properly represent employees in the affected business areas, and

- Have your candidature seconded by a colleague in one of the departments recorded as likely to be impacted by the potential redundancies, and

- Be available to personally attend consultation meetings, and

- Confirm with your manager that you will be seeking election as an employee representative and must be available for these duties if elected, and

Submit a completed nomination form to the People Help Desk in Reading for receipt on/before specified date and time.

6.2.4 Voting process

A list of candidates will be sent to the home address of those employees in each business area, together with a reminder of the process and a ballot paper. Each person has one vote against the full list of candidates and all votes are returned to the People Helpdesk.

Candidates will be informed of whether or not they have been selected by telephone and the final list of employee representatives will be communicated to all employees.

6.2.5 Elected employee role

He will be required to attend a briefing meeting. The meeting will:

- Allow him to understand the "ABC" wide process and specifically how your his area is impacted

- Confirm the responsibilities and jurisdiction of the role

- Provide guidance on how best to fulfil his role.

Following the meeting he will be given a briefing pack to remind him of the details from the meeting.

6.2.6 Employee Representative Nomination Form

Name:	
Business Unit:	
Department:	
Band:	
Contact telephone number:	

Please explain

- **Why you seek election as an employee representative AND**

- **What you believe qualifies you for this role.**

This information will be provided to colleagues during the election process to aid their decision to vote for candidates. Continue on a separate page if necessary but please restrict your comments to 300 words.

Name of seconder:	
Business Unit:	
Department:	
Signature of seconder	

I wish to participate in the election for employee representatives and confirm that I have read and will comply with the criteria to seek election.

Signed:	
Date:	

6.2.7 Role of redundancy committee

The elected employee representatives will attend a briefing meeting with business managers and HR managers. At this meeting the following information will be disclosed:

- The reasons for the proposed redundancies

- The numbers and descriptions of employees it is proposed to dismiss as redundant

- The total number of employees of any such descriptions employed at the establishment in question

- How the dismissals are to be carried out, taking account of any agreed procedure, including the period over which the dismissals are to take effect

- The method of calculating the amount of redundancy payments to be made to those who are to be dismissed

- The timeline for the proposed redundancies

- The principles of the selection criteria to be used and the process to be followed to select employees for potential redundancy

- Details of the process that will be followed to notify each affected employee of potential redundancy and the proposed termination arrangements

- This information will also be put up on "ABC" net for all employees to view.

6.2.8 Proposed selection criteria to be used

Core criteria will be used to ensure consistency across the establishments. These are:

- Skills and competencies
- Utilisation
- Performance
- Location and Mobility
- Length of Service

Within each establishment, there may be variations on the weightings given to these different components. Each establishment will determine the employee population that needs to be reduced (the pool) and will then review each employee in the pool against the specific selection criteria. This will produce a ranking of employees in the pool. Employees ranked below the threshold will be selected for potential redundancy.

6.2.9 Proposed method of carrying out the redundancies and calculating termination arrangements

The proposals will be discussed on how employees would be notified of potential redundancy, what would happen during the individual consultation period to support employees looking for alternative roles within "ABC" and what termination arrangements would be available in the event of termination of employment. Detail will be provided in the employee representative briefing pack that will be available on "ABC" net. The Company will be issued the draft letters to be used to inform employees of potential redundancy, the compromise agreement and final termination letter and a copy of the notifications for each establishment that will be sent to the DTI. The employee representatives will be reviewing the letters and termination arrangements in more detail.

The ex gratia payments can be made free of tax subject to the overall tax free exemption limit for termination payments of £30,000 per employee.

6.2.10 Outplacement Support

Mark Thomson from Right Management Consultants, "ABC'" company's chosen outplacement supplier, will be presented at the consultation meeting. Mark will be provided details about the range of outplacement support services to be provided to employees in the event of redundancies.

The employee representatives will be asked if some changes could be implemented to the level of service provided to employees so that there is no differentiation by band and age and that the duration of support is lengthened. Details of what this level of service would include will be discussed with Right Management Consultants.

6.3 Strengths

1. There is less chance an employee would be redundant.

2. There are alternative methods if redundancy occurs.

3. The procedure does not have any sex discrimination.

4. The procedure follows Equal Opportunities policy.

5. The procedure follows Country Government laws.

6. If redundancy is only alternative it formulates committee for all type redundancy discussion.

7. A redundant employee gets average £30,000.00 as redundant package in UK.

8. There are outplacement facilities available for a redundant employee.

9. The procedure involves every redeployee or redundant employee into discussion.

10. There is redundancy amount calculation method for every dismissed staff.

11. Dismissals taking account of any agreed procedure, including the period over which the dismissals are to take effect

12. Redundancy payments made to every dismissed staff

6.4 Weakness

- Present method is time taking.

- The HR department and managers need to put much time and enough resource.

- Present method does not talk about any specific method fro redundancy amount calculation.

- Present redeployment method is reactive not pro-active.

6.5 Recommendations

- It will be helpful for managers if it says specifically what are the redundancy criteria for what type of job roles.

- It will be helpful for managers if they know redundancy amount calculation method for different job roles.

- It should have proper forecast for benched employees because if the Company knows in advance how many will be benched for a certain period then it can forecast proper redeployment method for those benched employees.

- When redundancy is alternative method the Company can reduce salary level of all employees and keep the redundant staff for future redeployment. Because if company announce redundancy the Share value may be reduced in the market.

7 Key questions asked during "ABC" company interview

7.1 General

Is there any policy to determine employee needs what type of training for his development?

To what extent should policies be drawn up in consultation with staff?

How are unplanned and unexpected events dealt with?

How assessment been made of departments, team or individual contribution to their achievement?

7.2 The changing environment

What are the most significant external developments impacting on the company's recruitment and redeployment policies over the last six months?

What are the greatest threats and opportunities related to the achievement of deliverables, and how can these be addressed?

Has the policies changed regarding recruitment and redeployment or is it likely to change?

7.3 The business plan

Do the specified objectives and outputs in the plan correspond to the higher-level goals and policies of the department?

Have the departments' planned outputs for the review period been achieved?

Are the targets set challenging, specific and measurable? What performance indicators are being used to track progress?

7.4 The management of the department

How does the department deploy staff resources? Any changes needed?

What are the department's policies for developing staff? How are the support requirements for the area (such as financial management) being met?

7.5 Linkages

How does the department co-ordinate its work with other departments or other agencies? How are these linkages managed and what issues need to be addressed?

7.6   The process of planning

Was the plan prepared in a consultative/participative manner with department staff?

Are the arrangements set out in the plan for monitoring and review adequate?

8 "XYZ" Academy

In your capacity as the academy's personnel manager, write a report to George Thompson outlining the strengths and weakness of the academy's case on the forthcoming unfair dismissal case.

You should include an analysis on your chance of achieving a fair dismissal outcome and your recommendations on whether the case should be defended or an alternative course of action followed.

You are the academy based personnel manager, who provides education and training services to industry, commerce, and the general public. The academy employs 400 staff, but 50 working out of an annexe in Baldmare. Under the Baldmare manager, George Thompson, are three Programme Managers and an Office Manager. You provide an Advisory Service to the Baldmare management, who are expected to operate in accordance with the Academy's personnel policy manual.

Three years ago, Thompson recruited Robert Norbert as office Manager. Norbert was a 54 years old administrator who had been made redundant by a local insurance company. One reason for his selection was his knowledge of the insurance industry, as a number of the academy clients were insurance companies. Unfortunately, things have not worked out well. Thompson told you a year ago about Norbert's shortcomings – too many billing errors by his selection, occasional complaints by clients of his abrupt telephone manner, poor staff management and an un-cooperative attitude to other managers. You advised against immediate dismissal, pointing out that the disciplinary procedure required two written prior to dismissal and, at that time, none was on file. You also suggested that Norbert should be set specific performance targets.

Five weeks ago, Thompson phoned you to stay he's sacked Norbert. He explained that Norbert had not met targets he had been set for reducing billing errors. His attitude to other managers had also not improved. There had been a further complaint by a client of Norbert's unhelpful telephone manner. Thompson said these points had been put to Norbert in writing twice during the past year.

"But yesterday was the straw", Thompson went on. "Jane Yarrowby (one of the three programme managers) complained very strongly to me about Norbert's refusal to supply her quickly with details of client's records which she needed for an important meeting that afternoon. She told Norbert that the matter was urgent. Norbert said she would have to wait till tomorrow because he was too busy. I taxed Norbert about this and he said he had been checking for errors in accounts, which had to be sent out that afternoon. He added that Jane was always expecting him to drop other work to give her what he called fancy figures"

After this discussion Thompson had told Norbert he would be dismissed and issued him with an immediate dismissal letter. This said: "Following two occasions earlier this year when I had to advise you of my dissatisfaction with your work, and the incident yesterday when you refused to supply Mrs Yarrowby with data she needed for an important meeting. I have no alternative but to terminate your employment forthwith. You will be paid your contractual two months pay in lieu of notice."

You asked Thompson whether he had followed the disciplinary procedure and he said, "Yes, in essence if not to the letter." Norbert then appeal against dismissal and in accordance the procedure, the appeal was heard by Thompson himself. Norbert defence was:

- The performance targets were unrealistically high, given the poor quality of staff he had to employ because of the company's low office pay rates.

- Jane Yarrowby had not explained why she wanted the figures quickly – "she had just barged in and shouted."

- Management relationship involved two sides. The programme managers treated him as though he was an office boy, probably because they were young graduates who looked down on an unqualified older person.

- The client who complained had not been called as witness.

- He had not recognised Thompson's two earlier notes as a constituting formal written warnings.

- Procedures breached role of 'natural justice'.

Both of Thompson's earlier notes to Norbert read (after outlining his shortcomings and setting targets for reducing billing errors): "...Unless there is a significant improvement in your performance and attitudes, serious consequence may result.

At the appeal, Jane Yarrowby said she had not gone into detail about why she wanted the information quickly, but Norbert knew the client and should have realised the urgency. On the point about office salaries, you said that median market rates were paid, though there was a heavy demand for office staff in Baldmare.

- Thompson then confirmed Norbert's dismissal.

You have just received notification from the local industrial tribunal office that Norbert has registered a complaint of unfair dismissal, quoting the same points as in his company appeal. Thompson wants you to defend the case.

9 Annex 1

List of Strategy Statements Reviewed

- Managing Employees

- Managing Contractors

- Personal Details

- Absence

- Awards and Bonuses

- Benefits

- Career Framework

- Graduates & Apprentices

- Recruitment & Resourcing

- Terms and Conditions

- Training and Development

- HR Policies

10 Bibliography

No	Details
1.	Morris, S. & Willcocks, G. (1995) *Managing People: The Recruitment and Selection Process.* The Institute of Management, Pitman Publishing
2.	Armstrong, M. (1996) *Personnel Management Practice,* (6th edn), Kogan Page
3.	IRS (2001) *IRS Employment Review 739, 1 November 2001*
4.	CIPD (2000) *"Recruitment", Quick Facts series, Chartered Institute of Personal and Development, 2000, www.cipd.co.uk*
5.	Bennett, R. (1994) Managing People, (2nd edn). Kogan Page
6.	Cole, G. A. (1995) *Personnel Management*, (3rd edn). DP Publications Ltd
7.	http:\..\Redeployment\JCU - Redeployment and Redundancy Policy.htm

11 Index

ABC, 4, 6-7, 9

academic, 9

ACADEMY, 4, 7

Academy, 7

ACCEPTANCE, 6

Accountabilities, 5

achieved, 8

adapt, 10

address, 8

addressed, 8

adoption, 8

advertisement, 6

Advertising, 6, 10

against, 8

agencies, 10

aim, 8

all, 9

allocation, 8

also, 9

ALTERNATIVE, 6

alternative, 10

an, 7-9

Analyse, 6, 8

Analysing, 7

ANALYSIS, 4, 6-7

Analysis, 5

analysis, 5, 8-9

AND, 4-6

and, 3, 5-10

ANNEX, 4, 7

Annex, 9

annexure, 9

anonymous, 9

applicants, 10

applications, 6, 10

APPROACH, 5

approach, 9

Appropriate, 5

are, 8-10

areas, 9

arrangements, 6-7, 10

As, 8

as, 8-10

ASKED, 4, 7

asked, 9

ASSESS, 6

assess, 8

Assessing, 10

Assessment, 6, 10

AT, 4

At, 9

ATTRACT, 6

attract, 5

ATTRACTING, 5

Attracting, 10

attributes, 10

Avighna, 3

BACKGROUND, 5

background, 8

Bank, 6

based, 5, 8

be, 7-9

been, 9

Behavioural, 5

benefit, 9

BENEFITS, 6

benefits, 10

between, 8

BIBLIOGRAPHY, 4, 7

bibliography, 9

BOOK, 5

Book, 8-9

book, 3, 8-9

both, 9

Branding, 5

BUSINESS, 6-7

business, 8

But, 8

By, 1

by, 2, 9

calculating, 7

CANDIDATES, 5-6

candidates, 5, 10

carrying, 7

case, 7

catching, 5

central, 8

centred, 9

centres, 6, 10

certain, 8

Change, 7

change, 10

Changes, 7

CHANGING, 7

CHART, 5

CLARIFY, 6

Collective, 7

Committee, 6

committee, 7

companies, 8-9

COMPANY, 4, 6-7

Company, 8

company, 9-10

Competence, 5

competence, 5

competences, 5

COMPETENCIES, 6

competently, 10

concerns, 9

conclude, 8

conditions, 10

consultants, 6, 10

Consultation, 7

consultation, 8

CONTENT, 4, 6-7

Content, 5, 9

content, 8-9

CONTENTS, 4-5

Contents, 5

contextual, 9

continuous, 8

contracts, 10

control, 6

copy, 6

Copyright, 2

COST, 6

cost, 9

costs, 10

covered, 9

criteria, 5, 7

cross, 8

date, 9

daughter, 3

days, 1

dealt, 8

Deciding, 10

Decision, 6

defined, 8

DEFINING, 5

Defining, 10

DEFINITION, 5-6

Definition, 10

delivered, 9

demands, 10

DEPARTMENT, 7

departments, 8-9

depth, 9

derived, 9

DESCRIBE, 6

descriptions, 5, 10

Design, 6

details, 5

determined, 8

develop, 10

Development, 5

development, 8

devote, 3

different, 8-9

Diploma, 1

discussed, 9

discussions, 8

DISMISSAL, 6

Dismissal, 9

dismissal, 7

do, 10

documentation, 8

drawn, 8

DURING, 4, 7

during, 9

Educational, 6

effective, 8

effectively, 8

Elected, 7

elements, 8

Employee, 7

employee, 7

employing, 10

employment, 10

encourage, 8

end, 9

enhancing, 9

ensure, 8

ENVIRONMENT, 7

Environmental, 5

ESTABLISH, 6

establishments, 6

evaluating, 10

events, 8

evolving, 8

examples, 8

executive, 6

existing, 8

experience, 9-10

explores, 9

expression, 8

extent, 8

Eye, 5

factors, 5

Fair, 7

few, 5

finding, 10

FLOW, 5

FOCUS, 5

Focus, 8

focus, 8

focuses, 8

focusing, 8

follow, 6, 10

FOR, 4, 6-7

for, 7-10

Form, 7

form, 5

formal, 8

framework, 9

from, 9

future, 8

GAIN, 6

GENERAL, 7

GLANCE, 4

Good, 5, 8

good, 8, 10

has, 9

have, 9

highlighted, 8

How, 8

HR, 1

Human, 1

Identification, 10

identified, 8

IDENTIFY, 6

impact, 9

impacts, 9

implemented, 8

importance, 8

In, 1, 9

in, 1, 8-9

Include, 6

individual, 7

INDUCTION, 6

Induction, 6, 10

information, 6, 9

Initiative, 8

initiative, 8

inside, 10

insight, 9

intended, 8-9

intention, 8

inter, 6

INTERVIEW, 4, 7

Interview, 6

Interviewing, 5-6, 10

interviews, 5, 9

into, 9

intranet, 9

INTRODUCTION, 4-5

Introduction, 8

INVOLVING, 6

is, 8-10

ISBN, 2

issues, 8

It, 8

it, 9

JOB, 6

Job, 5-6

job, 5, 10

jobs, 10

KEY, 4, 7

key, 5, 8-9

Kumar, 2

last, 9

legislation, 8

LINKAGES, 7

linkages, 8-9

linking, 8

list, 9

listed, 9

LITERATURE, 4-6

Literature, 5, 9-10

literature, 9

longer, 8

made, 9

main, 8-9

Make, 8

Mala, 3

MANAGEMENT, 7

Management, 1, 8

management, 5, 8

manager, 7

managers, 9

material, 9

Mayukhi, 3

means, 8

media, 5-6

method, 7

METHODOLOGY, 5

methodology, 9

MONITORING, 6

more, 9

Motivating, 5

my, 3

NEED, 6

need, 8

needed, 8, 10

new, 8

Nomination, 7

number, 8

objectives, 8

obtain, 9

Obtaining, 10

occupational, 5

OF, 4-7

of, 5-10

OFFER, 6

Offer, 6

Offering, 10

offices, 8-9

official, 8

officials, 8

on, 8-9

operate, 8

or, 5, 10

order, 9

Organizational, 5

other, 8-9

OTHERS, 6

others, 6

out, 7-8

outlines, 9

Outplacement, 7

outside, 10

over, 8

Overall, 5

Part, 5

part, 8

particular, 8, 10

people, 10

Performance, 5

performance, 10

period, 8

Person, 5

personal, 5

personality, 10

Pijush, 1-2

place, 9

PLAN, 6-7

Plan, 6

PLANNING, 6-7

planning, 8-9

plus, 9

points, 5

policies, 8

policy, 8

Pool, 6

potential, 10

practice, 8-10

Pre, 6

Preliminary, 5

Preparation, 6

preparation, 9

Preparing, 10

presents, 9

priorities, 8

procedure, 9

PROCESS, 7

process, 7-10

produced, 8

Project, 9

Proposed, 7

provided, 9

published, 9

PURPOSE, 5

purpose, 5

QUESTIONS, 4, 7

questions, 8-9

reason, 7

RECOMMENDATIONS, 6-7

recommendations, 8-9

RECRUITMENT, 4-6

Recruitment, 6, 9-10

recruitment, 5, 8, 10

REDEPLOYMENT, 4, 6-7

Redeployment, 6, 9

redeployment, 8

redundancies, 7

REDUNDANCY, 6-7

Redundancy, 9

redundancy, 7

REFERENCE, 5

reference, 8

References, 6

references, 9-10

regard, 8

regarding, 8

related, 8

relatively, 8

Representative, 7

representative, 7

REQUIRED, 6

requirement, 6

REQUIREMENTS, 5

requirements, 10

Requisition, 5

Research, 9

Resource, 1

resource, 8

Responsibilities, 5

Retraining, 6

REVIEW, 4-6

Review, 8, 10

review, 5, 9

reviewed, 9

Reviewing, 10

reviews, 9

ROLE, 6

Role, 7

role, 7-8

Salary, 5

search, 6

Secondment, 6

Secondments, 7

Section, 9

section, 8-9

see, 9

SELECT, 6

Selected, 5, 9

selected, 9

SELECTING, 6

Selecting, 10

SELECTION, 4-6

Selection, 5-6, 9-10

selection, 7, 10

Sell, 5

Sen, 1-2

senior, 9

set, 8

sheet, 6

should, 8

Sifting, 6, 10

SKILLS, 6

skills, 10

SMI, 8

son, 3

sources, 9-10

specification, 5

specifications, 5, 10

staff, 8

Stages, 5

stages, 10

statement, 9

STATEMENTS, 4, 6-7

statements, 5, 8-9

steps, 8

still, 8

Strategic, 8

strategic, 8-9

strategies, 8

STRATEGY, 4, 6-7

Strategy, 8-9

strategy, 5, 8-9

STRENGTHS, 6-7

strengths, 5, 9

STRUCTURE, 5

structure, 9

studied, 9

study, 9

successfully, 10

Support, 7

term, 8

termination, 7

TERMS, 5

terms, 8, 10

Testing, 10

tests, 6

that, 8

THE, 5-7

The, 7-10

the, 5-10

their, 8, 10

These, 9

these, 8

they, 8

This, 9

this, 3, 9

those, 9

Three, 9

three, 9-10

Through, 8

through, 8

throughout, 9

Timing, 5

TO, 6

To, 8

to, 3, 5, 7-10

took, 9

towards, 8-9

training, 6

Transfer, 7

type, 7

Types, 6

unexpected, 8

unplanned, 8

up, 6, 8, 10

use, 8

used, 7, 9

useful, 6

Using, 6, 10

various, 9

view, 6

Voting, 7

was, 9

WEAKNESS, 6-7

weakness, 5, 9

were, 8-9

what, 8

which, 8-9

wife, 3

will, 8-9

with, 8-10

Work, 5

workforce, 7

would, 8

Write, 6

XYZ, 4, 7